PERFECTION

PERFECTION:

10 YEARS OF LOVE

A COLLECTION OF POETRY

BY

JORDAN LITTMAN

PERFECTION: 10 YEARS OF LOVE

Copyright © 2021 Jordan Littman

ISBN: 9798743231188

Dedication

this book is dedicated to
Numbers, Wordplay and **Love**
and to
The Woman
who means more to me
than all of them combined

Note to the Reader

This book is **NOT** about perfection. It is **NOT** about perfect people. It is **NOT** about a perfect relationship.

It is about humans. It is about love. It is about the small moments, the gentle gestures, the difficult hardships, and yes, the imperfections, that can make a relationship feel perfect.

I hope that you enjoy reading it and that one of this book's imperfections feels perfect to you.

With love,

Jordan Littman

Table of Contents

Prologue

Perfection: 10 Years of Love

10 (The World Is Binary)

the world is binary

thin, elegant *Ones*
standing proud and t
                        a
                        l
                        l
oozing positivity
through pristine pores
controlling cosmic energy
strength abounding
astounding even the universe

beside them
cold, empty *Zeroes*
forever surprised
mouths   a g a p e
praying for something
important to say
instead, they sit
atop crumbling walls
mumbling mute *w h i s p e r s*
into the abyss
slowly teetering
towards the edge

the world is binary

lightness looms
through darkened doorways
through looking glasses
half-empty and half-full
immaculate and shattered
tinted and rose-coloured
with every decision
both binary and infinite

the world is binary

moments stay or they go
moments fade or they grow
they take root, they spread
they infiltrate hearts and head
they are nurtured with suns and shades
until those moments sprout decades

the world is binary

a single word misplaced
corrupting code
sending the whole world   c
                          r
                           a
                            s
                             h
                              i
                              n
                              g

                        down

Jordan Littman

the world is binary

long days drowning
in pedestrian pools
the endless need to be   *on*
searching for the place

           where you can be yourself
searching for the place

           where you can truly belong
searching for the place

           where your puzzle pieces fit
searching for the place

           where you can finally be

        off

the world is binary

like picking petals
she loves me
she loves me not
she loves me
she loves me not
she loves me?

the world is binary

so in this tale
all about 10
everything is
all about two
two humans
two lovers
two souls
that live happily
~~ever after~~   *[ERROR: future unknown]*

1

We Are

This story begins before there was we
In a time before there was a you or a me
In a time when there was only he and she
Two strangers searching the streets

Searching for love, searching to connect
Searching for homes that couldn't be wrecked
Searching for moments, their cause and effect
Two strangers stuck in their seats

And so…

She sat waiting.
He sat waiting.
They sat waiting.

They sat in different rooms, in different houses.
They sat in different places, at different times.
They sat, barely even satisfying the definition of they.
At this point, the only thing they had in common was
    that they were waiting.

They waited.
They waited and waited and waited.
They waited until their bones cracked and cricked,
As the clocks tocked and ticked,
All the while gazing
Through windows blocked and bricked,
Hiding the forecasted futures
They'd concoct and predict.

But…

Who is this he?
Who is this she?
Who is this pair destined to become we?
Let us turn the pages and see.

She

she is fresh popcorn
from movie theatres
with extra butter

she is the parade of dolls
that helped her sleep
and the ones
that kept her up at night

she is the gifted rocks
collected with love
undeterred by empty pockets
sparking joy
in cold lake water
rekindling fires
on maine beaches in may

she is the ellis thighs
perfect for conversations with cousins
and horseback riding
and scaling fences
and childbirth

she is the four questions
and a dozen more questions
when four won't suffice
never satisfied with anything less

than a perfect understanding
of an imperfect world

she is made of full body crunches
of frustration
of love
craving the closeness
of friendships found
in moments behind sofas
waiting to scream *surprise!*

it's time to scream, because…

she has arrived

she is here

she is

He

he is computers
from apple
and noise-cancelling headphones

he is the silent room with a closed door

he is the manufactured tulips
the manicured trees
the forest labelled like tupperwared leftovers

complaining when they leave and forgetting when they
    stay
the names that begin with j's and m's

he is
apples with honey
and
ketchup with honey
from
don't be late
to
you're my best boy and i love you

he is the phantom holiday congregations
where they hummed familiar tunes
for lack of meaningful words to sing
the feeling like broccoli

the cries for attention
and the dull butter knives
that couldn't excise the frustration

he is the basketball courts
and skipped lectures
that brought them together
and the college towns
that tore them apart
the brooding green eyes that told him
he was truly connected
and yet truly alone

he grew tired of living alone
so in that moment
he decided to stop

he has arrived

he is here

he is

Her Dream

she always dreamed of
falling asleep
and
waking up
beside someone
searching for safety
in sleep cycles shared
with the one
who will be there in the morning
to listen to her dreams

His Dream

he always wanted to
wake up
in a dream that lasted
until he fell asleep
to feel the restful
embrace of daylight
and to consider the night
as time created
simply for preparation

Another Him I (Time I)

she asked him for the time
he said *sorry, i don't have it*
she pointed at his watch
he pointed at the door

she asked him for his love
he said *fine, i'll need it back though*
he threw his icy heart
she froze there evermore

Another Him II (Stardust)

she sprinkled stardust
from her eyes
emitted with
every tear

he *made* her cry
at each sunrise
so *the world*
would fill with cheer

slowly the stardust
trickled tender
she withered
all the while

he did not know
in all her splendour
stardust flowed stronger
with each *smile*

Another Him III (Shade)

he promised to be your umbrella
protecting you from the rain
he only showed up on sunny days
smothering you with shade

Searching for Answers, Finding More Questions

                    he was
          heartily   waiting,
        hating   that
                          every
                          time
                        he sat
                        gazing
                        at the
                      night
                    sky,
                  the
                  stars
                  only
                sorted
                into

            question
            marks

Casting Shadows

she saw a world full of shadows
never realizing she was the sun

Observing Shadows

he saw a world full of shadows
knowing that eventually he would find the light

2

We Meet

Now, we have met mister and we have met miss
Our two star-crossed heroes, searching for bliss
Determined to climb out of the abyss
To take their place on life's stage

Ready for lights and ready for action
Ready to learn the laws of attraction
Ready to sit in pure satisfaction
Together, coming of age

It was on this evening that
                                    something so
            surprisingly
                              ordinary
                  happened.

She became you.
He became me.
She and he hopped out of the hypothetical,
Abandoned the anonymous,
And were reborn into reality.
But, with only one you
And with only one me,
There was only one way that
We would become we.

And so…

I got ready.
You got ready.
We got ready.

We got ready for a party, a gathering of peers,
Connected through fragments, woven by a web of
    spacetime,
Possibly for the sole purpose of presenting us
With the presence of possibility and purpose.
On the surface, this meeting was inconsequential,
Though the consequences radiate through the pages of
    this book,
Leaving the reader with a far greater understanding
Of the importance of chance encounters
Than was evident to what would become us
On what was a sweltering summer eve.

For it was…

Twenty-Ten, Ninth of July
A fun-loving girl met a confident guy
The first time that we would see eye to eye
Your gaze met mine with a contented sigh

Under This Sky

under this sky
your eyes met mine
sapphires glimmer
in stars that shine
from beads of sweat
glistening skin
reflecting tides
the moon draws in
gravity pulls
raw magnetism
your heart attracts
my pessimism
close encounters
and then good-bye
a world was born
under this sky

Waiting for the Crash

you came into my life
a burning bolide
in a flash of fury

lighting up
                    my skies
heating up
                    my heart
spicing up
                    my life

and i just stood there
waiting for the
c r a s h

Stop Sign

even from across the room,
i could clearly read the bold lettering
on your face, flushing red with the mildest
of compliments, as if it were impossible that
they *STOP* could
define you.
then your
eyes met
mine and i knew that i had to stop. i
looked both ways before crossing the
room in order to reach my

d
e
s
t
i
n
a
t
i
o
n

Meeting - A Sonnet

content with carnal notes that men oft sing
misplacing maps, i settled for a chase
as hare, i ran til morning bells did ring
awoke to catch myself in lust's embrace

this weary journey brightened next to you
your virgin lips spoke only in love song
reflecting strangers' eyes in perfect hue
through windows, joyful paths where we belong

as dali's clocks did melt in summer heat
drips dropping down our twisted hour glass
that never should our souls have chanced to meet
in parallel our destinies to pass

praise sorcerers' distractions cast in light
that led me off the path from you that night

Destiny Became Impatient

our footsteps fell on sidewalks slow
we walked the ways we knew to go
no need to rush or pick up pace
slack strings began to interlace
paths that crossed would surely bind
your heart to mine, a love to find

destiny became impatient
tautly tying us adjacent
your blue connected to my green
a calm came over, so serene
we could not hide from destiny
she brought you here to be with me

Fairy Tale Fantasies

all those times
when the stars misaligned
and the tarot cards turned
and my palms creased just wrong
though i didn't believe in any of it

through those times
i always believed in you

sometimes
you would enter through dreams
a powerful princess
taming my dragons
gracing me with one glance
gracing me with one dance

most times
i awoke alone

then there was the time
my dreams came true

Collections

i collected hockey cards

and forgot where i put them

i collected coins

and forgot where i put them

i collected words
        and lectures
        and formulae

and forgot where i put them

when i found you
i was searching for
a collection of phone numbers
                to forget

                i forgot to keep searching

Monkey Bars

i reached for you
like monkey bars
full of bravado
certain
i would
fall

Wish Chip

you found me
misshapen
crumpled
looking inward at myself
and you were ecstatic to stop
crinkling through the bag
and i was lucky
that you loved
wish chips

Another Time I

in another time
we may have met as children
two dollar teeth
missing from playground smiles
searching for ants
to tickle your pale, sun-kissed arms
unflattering facades
for future people
who could only grow together
and
who could only grow apart

Another Time II

in another time
we may have met as teenagers
stray coarse hairs
crackling voices
pheromones pretending
to reveal the truth about love
left only with scars of disillusionment
scratched into green and blue irises
a universal truth
all our own
heartache brushed off
as growing pains

Another Time III

in another time
we may have met as seniors
depressed divorcees
searching for meaning
craving companionship
old dogs learning new tricks
to walk in step
to cease barking inconsequential insults
as we count the sunsets
through the rearview mirror

Another Time IV

in another time
we may have never met at all
the cruel curve
of time and space
shooting our souls
in divergent directions
destined to dwell
in a silent world without song
in a colourless autumn landscape
focused on trees
there is no forest
in oblivion

Jordan Littman

10 (Time II)

you asked me for the time
i said *i'll be there in ten minutes*
when i arrived in eight
you gasped *why are you so late?*

i looked down at my watch
and asked *did i keep you waiting?*
you looked into my eyes
and smiled *only my whole life*

Summer Playlist

that summer
we exchanged
songs
every note
the key
to our hearts
every lyric
the secrets
to our souls
every beat
the rhythm
of our destinies
bursting forth
from subaru speakers
on the road
to somewhere

that summer
we listened

that summer
we loved

.

Peanut Butter Memories

the memory of our first kiss
sticks to the roof of my mouth
like peanut butter
spread by the tip of your tongue
tickling my lips into a smile

3

We Journey

Through summer days, we journeyed on
The tie-dyed skies burned bright neon
The moonlit nights were halcyon
We'd found our place

But just as soon as love did start
You packed your clothes and took my heart
Europe-bound, forced to depart
Through time and space

And so...

We separated.
We waited.
We commiserated about the times we were elated.
Had all those feelings dissipated?
Or were we simply devastated?
Concentrated on the complicated?
Frustrated by love, belated,
Desecrated by distance dictated?
With a knife, serrated, situated in our chest,
We calculated length of life and advocated for the test of
     time.
Though we hated
Being segregated and isolated,
Our love was not invalidated,
But accelerated.
The hours we communicated
Proved to us that we were slated
To be affiliated.

So we dated.
We dated and dated and dated,
Until the nights and days faded and amalgamated into
    an ocean of love.
Though the ocean still divided, we resided beside each
    other
In hearts and minds, one and the same.
Two of a kinds are winning this game.
Whether in Sweden or Portugal or the dark side of the
    moon,
We knew we would come back stronger, when you
    returned in June.

And so…

The voyage must lead to a place up ahead
The reader must read, 'til the story is read
The journey unravels, let's pull at that thread
And sift through the travels, where our love was bred

Distance

you

may be far away
exploring lost cities
tourist towns
meeting friends foreign to

me

despite the distance
i have never felt
closer to someone
the miles melting away
leaving our souls

e
n
t
w
i
n
e
d

together

My Strength

absence makes the heart grow fonder
my heart can't take it any longer
someone call my first responder
like samson's hair, she makes me stronger

since she left, i'm becoming weaker
my sermons delivered by mute preacher
dark horizons looking bleaker
until i draw the strength to reach her

i know, one day, she will return
bellowed chants and blown ram's horn
my heart no longer needs to yearn
my strength returns, i am reborn

Oxygen I

love is oxygen
the essence of life
the secret of survival
invisible, taken for granted
until you sit alone
floating in orbit
looking down at a distant world below
lacking the very connection you require
lacking the one thing you desire
and with an empty chest
both heart and lungs
starving for attention
there's nothing left but to close your eyes
and let your frozen tears flow

Oxygen II

love is oxygen
in a moment beside her
rushing in to fill the vacuum
expanding every notion of fulfillment
ballooning until our love is one
with the universe
and there we sit
on the edge of existence
amnestic astronauts
blissfully unaware
breathing deeply
forevermore

Celestial

you are a star
not because you sparkle

                though you do

but because despite the distance
you still light my way

you are a sun
not because you shine

                though you do

but because despite the distance
you warm my heart

you are a moon
not because you're bright

                though you are

but because despite the distance
your gravity shapes my tides

you are celestial
not because you are out of this world

                though you are

but because despite the distance
my world only exists in you

True Love Ways

when you leave
there is still home
when you breathe
i'm not alone
when you move
the music plays
all to prove
our true love ways

Your Air

i inhale air that was once in you

when i remember to b r e a t h e
when my lungs are aching from lacking

when i need to visit
the warmth of your heart
the sweet scent of your lips
the calming energy that stains every atom

even when the mile markers taunt us
i feel you close with every breath
and i know that no ocean
can keep our gusting winds apart

Senses I (A Single Touch)

footsteps falling on foreign soil
as i fall into your arms
catching my breath
in the crisp and salty air
a single touch
brings dreams to life
clearing the fog from
portuguese skies
the sand exfoliating your feet
calloused from a lifetime
of running from yourself
now found
in giggles
syrup smiles
and
a home
miles from home

Indiana

without indiana
my north would be untrue
not even mariana
comprehends the depths of you
no storm in the savanna
could quench a thirst so dry
endless pranayama
would miss your breath float by

Peaks

there was often sadness in reaching the peak
knowing there was nowhere to go but down
yet i am glad that i kept climbing
for you have a mountain range to explore

You Are a Star

you scurry down the stairs
up the door
through the mail slot

freedom at last

your light emanates
a shining orb
lighting up the midnight porch
casting fearful shadows
from the cacophony
of hand-painted wind chimes

freedom greeted you at the door
like a long lost lover
with a twinkle of flirt in their eye
and a sprinkle of hesitation on their brow
this moment seemed to linger
in every sleepless slumber
and every dreamful day
but now it seems to pass so swiftly

suddenly you reach the road
unsure of how you arrived
another journey travelled
yet forgotten
lost to the travesty of time

the street remains quiet
even the night is sleeping

you gaze above
the dark canvas
the new moon teasing
its lightbulb flickering
before blissfully burning out

you begin to rise
your light expands to vastly fill the void
with the tranquility of a star
and the confidence of a sun
and with barely a thought
to the darkness that was
you take your place
in the cosmos

My Yellow Brick Road

through the gloomy window
where clouds print pouts
and roundabouts
impede us as we go

you line the path
of yellow bricks
with treats and tricks
that always make me laugh

Elastic Hearts

the world pulled on our elastic hearts
wearing us thin
until the tension grew too strong

we could have snapped
broken
torn
forlorn

instead
we were launched back
into each other's arms
with such intensity
that our skin fused

held forever
by our crazy glue love

.

4

We Arrive

Then our footsteps settled down
We found ourselves on steady ground
Our home bodies were homeward bound
To a place that we could share

We packed our bags and then our truck
Didn't fully comprehend our luck
Glued so close, yet felt unstuck
To live, to dream, to dare

I was here.
You were here.
We both were   here.

The first true inauguration of we
A grand culmination in its simplicity
A perfect demonstration of what we were meant to be
The overdue celebration of our unity

Would it meet the expectations
Set by months of declarations
Of a love requiring patience?
Was it time for congratulations?
'Fore, we lived off banter and flirtations.
Now, the time to build foundations
With strength to weather all frustrations
That come with lasting, close relations.
Though we both had reservations,
Due to former situations,

Where the complex complications
Could not be met with reparations,
It never stopped the affectations,
The freely flowing admirations.
For when we pair, the combinations
Turn our days into vacations.

Therefore…

We had a new start, a moment of arrival
We contented our heart, so joyous, convival
After time apart, fighting for survival
We've now reached the part for our love's spring revival

New Tenant

windows boarded
glass is shattered
dust collects on
all that mattered
sunlight exits
shadow enters
memories
evicted renters
faded portraits
bare survival
i, abandoned
then, your arrival

Prime Numbers

my life was in its prime
when i was twenty three
i was invincible
the only factor, me
you proved i shouldn't dwell
on things that would divide
splitting rendered futile
once our love had multiplied

Senses II (New Love Smell)

i tried to keep your new love smell
hanging it from my rearview mirror
spritzing it on my neck and wrists
infusing it into incense
filling my home with your pheromones

but the distance was too far
and my sense of smell too weak
i've always been allergic to missing you
so, as the parts per million dwindled
i could no longer feel you near
luckily, that was the end of the year

you rushed back into my presence
the essence overwhelming
the new love smell had aged
like fine wine and whiskey
with notes complex, earthy, yet otherworldly
a scent renaissance, wise and strengthened

i imprinted the spirit in my mind
preparing for the return of the allergies
to sniff on rainy days with cool breeze
teary eyes squeezed mid-sneeze
but the *just-in-case* felt insincere
insecure, steeped in fear

so i threw out the memory of new love smell
the same day you discarded your old key
to live with me
there's no need for the memories
when we wake every morning
bathing in the aroma of fresh coffee and old love

.

10 (Perfect Ten)

hey there! i just need to say
i'd give you a perfect ten
excuse my superficial words
but there are no perfect men
i see what's on your surface
and pretend to understand
an iceberg hides and bides its time
so elegant and grand
what gives me right to criticize?
what gives me right to rate?
when i can hardly comprehend
what you have on your plate
perhaps no man is worthy
instead i should crowdsource
yet every time i look around
they marvel at your force
but beholder begets beauty
and perfection is the same
so i create the rules this time
you're playing in my game
so since you have a perfect heart
bursting forth with kindness
and since you have perfect eyes
that thrust me out of blindness
and since you have the perfect smile
flooding me with joy
then you must be a perfect ten
and i, your unworthy boy

Coffee

your coffee stained lips
give me the energy of a full cup

Perfection

you are only imperfect
in every way
you allow
yourself to think

you are only imperfect
in every way
your mouth
speaks in lip sync

you are only imperfect
in every way
you dream
to be another

you are only imperfect
in every way
your imperfections
take cover

you are only imperfect
in every way
you colour
inside the lines

you are only imperfect
in every way

you sit
and count the signs

you are only imperfect
in every way
the reflecting
glass can see

you are simply perfect
in every way
so set
your imperfections free

Samaritan

i fell in love with your shoulder
draped with soft samaritan's skin
on wintery days when i'm colder
the crackling fires warm from within

on the rainiest days, its sun
creates deserts from teardrop lakes
a pillow top, second to none
at soothing my deepest heartaches

my maw agape, awestruck, i found
this shoulder attached to its friends
while exploring your holy ground
my soul delightfully transcends

Your Masterpiece

control me like your canvas
cover me with your plentiful palette
positive purples
delicate pinks
joyous yellows
i want to feel the rush
of your watercolours
brushing against my skin
i want your paint to permeate
every inch of me
until i am completely transfigured

thanks to you
i will become
your masterpiece

Lost Time

we walk one way streets in reverse
hands entwine, fingertips converse
hands of time spin withershins
clutching earth to cease the spins
fishing from our front porch mast
reeled in sunsets shine everlast
anything to prevent the pain
of losing more time with you again

Dissection

i took my scalpel blade
to your deceptive paper skin
uncovering all the secrets
hiding there within
through fascia, bone and muscle
through your glowing heart
pumping joy into the world
was only just the start
as i dissected deeper
unsure of what i'd find
suddenly mesmerized
a discovery, one of its kind
i'd add it to the textbooks
i'd make it my life's work
to show the world the beauty
of this precious little quirk
i tried hard to describe it
but words didn't seem to fit
bliss, nirvana, happiness
all seemed inadequate
so instead i put my pen down
and my scalpel blade down too
there was no need for accolades
there was only need for you

Everything

the look in her eyes
brought everything back

5

We Connect

Our love grows stronger every day
Like flowers blooming late in May
Combatting every shade of gray
Hues splashing on our lives

We wake each morning in a daze
With eyes that glow in morning rays
Hands that touch and hold and graze
Our connection builds and thrives

We fit

           together

    like:

Flowers and soil, sharing in the beauty of time spent
    soaking in tears of joy
Clouds and rain, forces of nature unmasking our shared
    identity
Lips, dancing, synchronous and sensual, the
    choreography of connected hearts
Fingers, sharing a warm and cozy glove
Dawn and dusk, the dutiful days marching always
    onwards
Sun and moon, I'll follow you wherever you go,
    reflecting your light
Finished sentences, prepositions laced beautifully
    between subjects
Completed thoughts, your voice trailing mine until the
    perfect punctuation

Then…

Life moved forward as a dream
We moved forward as a team
Warming hearts, releasing steam
Where glaciers stood, a flowing stream

Change of Pace

i
always
prided
myself
on
being
succinct
but with you, i want to let every line linger a little longer
sometimes repeating lines
over and over and over and
over and over and over and
over and over and over and
over again
even adding extra consonants for
effffffffffffffffffffffffffffffffffffffffffffffect
anything to ensure that our story never ~~ends~~

Palms

imprinted palms
press love through soft skin
casually caressing
the serious trapped within
lost tombs
i hope to never find
stay and play
forever in my mind

Questions

you question whether
i truly love you
or whether i simply
love not being alone

there is no distinction
when every moment
spent without you
is imbued with

isolation

Coke

i want to love you like a coke
and feel you sizzle on my lips

Senses III (Sight)

i saw you today
and
it made me wonder
what my eyes did
every other time
they gazed upon you

Rest

rest your head on me tonight
let's dream our way into
tomorrow's eternity

Eye to Eye

eyes reflecting me
reflecting locks without a key
reflecting jail, reflecting free
reflecting truth i cannot see

eyes reflecting scars
reflecting further from the cars
reflecting earth, reflecting mars
reflecting truth beyond the stars

eyes reflecting eyes
reflecting off serene blue skies
reflecting lows, reflecting highs
reflecting truth beneath disguise

Grape I

a grape lies sleeping
upon my gentle tongue
thin-skinned, weeping
sweetest notes unsung
crisp, autumn dew
a flare for surprise
deeply deja vu
a scent to recognize
caressing curves
dare not to bite
calming nerves
i'll keep you safe tonight

Eavestrough

i'll drape from your neck, to collect all your rain
when lassitude threatens your tear-soaked terrain
in return, please ensure that my leaves get unclogged
i'm no good at collecting, when i drape water-logged

Invade My Flesh

invade my flesh
i'll open the doors
no need to hide
in a wooden horse
you comfort me
you heal all my sores
we'll be as one
i'm forever yours

Sun and Moon

you compliment
and call me bright

though i am but a moon
reflecting your light

.

Saviour

her gentle smile and risibility
lift him from invisibility
reinstating his ability
to brave the light again

6

We Fight

But it's not always wine and roses
For love, untended, decomposes
Perhaps contentment presupposes
Complacency

Yes, there are times with boiling blood
And jeers and sneers all caked in mud
Kindness drowns in a raging flood
We're lost at sea

We are simply living our lives

      when

                    suddenly

  it hits…

SMACK!
We brace for the attack.
Our world burns red, before it starts to fade to black.
We try to backtrack,
Flip the scripts like a flapjack.
Focus on the things we have and forget all those we lack.
But every wisecrack
Must be met with a comeback.
They play back
Over and over, a vicious soundtrack.
It's payback.
Once, we sat there laidback.
Now we only lie in anger, guess we're insomniac.
Searching for the right words hidden in the haystack,

But every word we speak cuts deeper than a lumberjack.
Even our fallen forest can't stop us as we bushwhack.
With every hack,
A counterattack.
Brains buzzing from the feedback.
Eventually our fires fade and fizzle out the smokestack.
Come the morning we'll sit puzzled, reaching for an ice
    pack.

Because…

We live to fight another day
We yearn to light up a new way
We take a right, but are led astray
Will the dark of night ever fade away?

Elements of Heartache

darkness
              lands
on stormy
              seas
hearts on
              fire
lost in
              breeze

Infuriating I

it must have been
infuriating
to travel the entire ocean
searching for the wave
that would carry you home
only to be carried back to sea
by my angry riptide

Wishes I

when someone hands you their worn fragile heart
scarred by your dragon claws
and gives you another chance to protect it
it is your solemn duty
not to throw it in the trash fire
screaming you are not worthy of my love

- things I wish I knew then

Bights and Fights

fingertips nip at your bights and curves
riptide forcing me from your shores
drowning deep in our fights and words
the scars in my head counting scores
remember the time with the sights and birds
the soundscape surrounded our souls
the mellowing music our nights deserved
were siren songs taking their tolls

True Purposes

you cry
i scream
the cycle continues
until we learn
that our eyes
are meant for
connecting gazes
and our mouths
for loving whispers

Infuriating II

it must have been
infuriating
to finally find the
seashell
that completed your collection
only to find that
your mermaid voice
would not echo back
no matter how close
you pressed your ear to mine

Petals

please do not peel
my skin like petals

you can count on me
without the pain

why do you force me
to answer in screams?

why do you bobble
at the boom in my voice?

should i stay silent at the sight
of my skin piled on your floor?

or should i sweep them up
to complete another chore?

i will simply pick them

    one

          by

               one

and glue them into scars
an eternal mark of my fragility
a painful reminder of your power
               over
               me

Bridges I

how many bridges can i burn
by doing the right thing
in the wrong way
by trying to give love
but only giving pain

Speaking Apart

sometimes i get the feeling
that we are simply talking
past each other.

sometimes i get the feeling
that we combine
into one mind.

when my contributions
are not valued
then i suffer.

each day marvelling
at all the wonders
we designed.

we plan. we perform.
but we never stop to

listen.
to the sounds
of tides as they

contemplate
our ebb and flow.
never pausing to be

still.
silence, soothing silence
allowing it to fill

us.
i hope that
we still know

our hearts.
our heads.
our souls.

give love.
get love.
#communicationgoals

Favourite Song

you are my favourite song
but sometimes i still forget your words

Heart Attack

acrid air, through carnivorous teeth
a strangling stare, a noose from wreath
labouring lungs, lugubrious breaths
heart, beat down, at dangerous depths
aching cries, pierce chest, pierce back
body writhing from your heart attack

Volcano

bubbles below the surface
waiting to erupt
i'd play some calming music
but the files are corrupt
i would take a few deep breaths
but my chest is getting tight
the anger spirals fiercely
the beginning of a fight

Flames

i thought that if i could walk through your flames
i would emerge a phoenix
ready for my new life to begin

but my feet are still blistered and blackened
my eyes are soaking in steam
and your ash still collects on my skin

7

We Love

Time again our love endures
From biting lips, a kiss that cures
From fighting notes, fresh overtures
Fill our days with song

Cold shoulder silence won't impede
Quiet comfort won't mislead
Our booming symphony guaranteed
To prove that we belong

Through

         our

  journey,

      we

   discovered

          that

Love is…

… a warm fleece blanket on a cold winter night.
… a mountain we'll never tire of climbing.
… a diamond, hard and precious.
… finding hidden messages in birdsong.
… the nuance in every silence.
… writing poetry at 3am, so I can speak to you even
    while you sleep.
… waking up the dreamers inside us.
… not needing to define it.

And then…

We hear the message, loud and clear
Our smiles presage a joyful year
Words become vows, when held sincere
Communication allows our love to reappear

Hot off the Presses

you think i'll tire of you
that i'll get bored
that i'll trade you in
like i do with

                  my gadgets
                  my car
                  my hobbies

but i could never wake up
without the warmth of
the newest edition of you
hot off the presses

Spinning

sing to me
you make my world spin
let me play you on repeat

Just Right

perfect conditions
twenty two degrees, sunshine
gentle breeze, your smile
making memories to save
us in dark, rain-soaked, cold nights

My Worst Enemy and My Best Friend

you are my worst enemy
no one else could be so inept
so incompetent
so utterly ineffectual
such that every befuddled attempt
to make me suffer
instead brings me joy
as if your only desire
is for me to succeed
to be content
to have a heart
filled with love
for my best friend

Gates of Heaven

if eyes are the windows to the soul
then yours are the gates of heaven

Yellow Zip

a yellow zip
a ray of light
a warm lip
in the night
centred, present
full of hope
joyful, godsent
my yellow rope

Ashtray

i wish to sit upon your table
empty and purposeless
just to be
close to you

and though i crave
the sweet ash
you leave behind
i can't bear to watch
you *puff, puff, puff*
filling yourself with
lies, hate, hurt
poisoning your perfection

so if i tempt you terribly
please move me to your attic
    with the cobwebs
        and the graphic tees
            and the memories
at least, i'll still have
    the sounds of the house
        bending to your will
            the air vent
                recycling your perfume
the winding staircase
    that connects us
        to collect dust
            for you
will always be enough

Senses IV (Silent Sounds)

our love is a silence
that contains
all of the words
we've ever said

in this silence
souls mould sounds
into sunset symphonies

in this silence
there is beauty
        comfort
        support
        passion
        respect
        happiness

in this silence
there is home

Out of Reach

searching for the perfect words
to describe you,
the participles always dangle
just out of reach

Astronaut

i am an astronaut
and you are the oxygen tank
i could never live without

10 (Belonging)

i look around and see me:

empty
like my pockets

empty
like the hole
at the centre of my chest

empty
like a *Zero*
praying for value

i look around and see you:

the source of power
around whom i am stronger

the centre of attention
around whom i am noticed

the important *One*
about whom books are written

i look around and see us:

10
in bed
bodies connected
cheeks to pillows
eyes to eyes

10
double digits
we are playing
in the big leagues

10
perfection
hand in hand
across the land

8

We Hurt

Day follows day, a cycle disenchanted
We begin to take our relationship for granted
Missing the slope until we stand slanted
The fall leaves scrapes and bruises

We try to cleanse but no peroxide
Can heal the cuts that hurt deep inside
Perhaps pain receptors, amplified,
Ensure that everyone loses

I hurt.
You hurt.
We both hurt
          each other.

SMACK, it hits again.
Anger swirling round and round, a savage hurricane.
It's more than we can ascertain,
This crumbling domain.
Once filled with joy, now our tears fill it with acid rain.
It's insane,
The levels of hate we can attain.
Remarks of romance turn to declarations of disdain.
I try to hold you close, so the passion will remain,
But as we try to cling together, we simply suffocate in
     cellophane.
Oh, the pain!
A pounding to the brain,
Like a never-ending migraine.
Will it wane?

Or will it sustain for all eternity?
What's there to gain from all this hurt in me?
I want to explain
How a human can act so inhumane,
But the boiling blood inside my vein
Make the explanations seem arcane.
There's bubbling rage inside of me, like poisonous
  champagne.
I try to abstain,
Try to pour it down the drain,
But when you complain,
I'm afraid I can't refrain.
It's the bane
Of our relationship, the cause of all our strain,
And if we can't restrain,
Then will all of this have been in vain?

For…

How can One and One be two
When I feel like Zero next to you?
When will my inner hero break through
To provide the support that I withdrew?

Atheist

you told me
i have a
god complex
and i lost all
faith in myself

If the Hourglass Breaks

if the hourglass breaks, who keeps time
my heart still aches, and the clocks won't chime
time stands still with you still on my mind
sands spill from me, brain logged offline
the grains stain the gravel, veins clogged with grime
painstaking travel, terrains tough to climb
prayin' for refuge, after the huge incline
if the fall doesn't kill me, you'll commit the crime

Grape II

a grape still remains
upon my lashing tongue
wrinkled, as life drains
from a body, still young
trapped by thrashing teeth
that swore to protect
that thin-skinned sheathe
windburned, wrecked
carried for a decade
a fruit i thought was mine
became bitter and afraid
no chance to turn to wine

Infuriating III

it must have been
infuriating
to find your soulmate
in a lost voyageur
pouring your heart
into every word of
affection
and discovering that
i could not
translate
your language of love

More Royal Than Purple

my heart is still tender
where you left a bruise
more royal than purple
more scars than tattoos
less painful than leaving
alone and recluse
never enough
for your baby blues

Wishes II

when someone confides in you their most fragile fears
it is your solemn duty
not to use them as weapons
each day
to attack
until there is no pain left inside
their broken armour

- things I wish I knew now

Fortress

you
        held me
        so softly
        that it only
took
        two years until
my
fortress
        crumbled
        into a puddle
        of tears
        on your shoulder

Wilting Flower

wilting now, my humble flower?

> your thirst remains unquenched

drink this tonic

> as i glower
> your tear-soaked soil's drenched

let me dry those fronds, you're crying

> evaporating breaths
> renegade eyes, falsifying

rejoice

> in flower deaths

Senses V (Can't Taste Sweet)

your salt-soaked tears melted on my tongue
drowning dark chocolate notes that were left unsung
savouring the pound of flesh
and the sour grapes that were not picked fresh
longing to return to your honey hips
but i can't taste sweet in this apocalypse

Emotions Form Erosions

tears tumble from her soul
carving canyons deep in her cheeks
emotions form erosions
erasing her gentle spirit
defacing her delicate smile
reaching for support
unleashing her inner beauty

A Step Behind

we walk the path again
same path
same partner
same leaves lying across the lawns
as the path forks
you steer right
always a step ahead
it's our way
the way we walk
a contract we signed in breath
tousled brown hair
atop a tall pedestal
you gaze down
while i gaze at you
you don't understand
the gusts of wind don't seem to blow you over
always in the eye of the twister
while it sweeps me off of my feet
walk with me again tomorrow
but walk a step behind

Bridges II

how many bridges can we burn
before we lose the road
that leads us
home

Scissors and Knives

don't love me, you'll hurt yourself
as scissors and knives fall off the shelf
crashing to the earth below
red teardrops will surely flow
a shattered heart, resounding pain
i hurt the one i love again

9

We Build

After the fight, comes the calm
We coat our wounds with healing balm
We reach for love with open palm
We solidify our bond

The more we learn, the more we grow
The more we live, the more we know
We see ourselves in tomorrow
And the years beyond

Until
                              only
        one
                                        question
              remains…

Will you…
        … dream with me every day?
        … search with me for an elusive forever?
        … walk with me on an endless journey?
        … breathe with me and fill our souls?
        … marry me?

And you said…
        … it would be a dream come true.
        … even if we never find it.
        … and if our legs tire, we'll simply take flight.
        … we'll never breathe alone again.
        … YES!

And so…

We now begin to plan ahead
And count the days until we wed
'Til gowns are worn and vows are said
'Til two lives fuse into one instead

Teacher

you teach me words i could never speak

           and hold their meaning true

you teach me notes i could never sing

           while keeping melody too

you teach me colours i could never paint

           and maintain their vibrant hue

you teach me love i could never share

           with anyone else but you

Megafauna

we are elephants
memories of the past
creating our future

we are mammoths
returning from extinction
to touch our tusks
just one more time

we are dinosaurs
our buried bones
unearthed entwined
scientists may mistake
your hands for mine

we are megafauna
terraforming tenderly
shaping it all
growing together
when we feel small

My Gift

every morning
i leave the house
entering the world with only one intention
to bring the world back home to you

every evening
i return home
empty arms, knuckles dragging on the floor
acutely aware that the world was here all along

Each Day

hello
　　hello again
　　we meet again each day
　　enlightened each day
　　by your shining smile
　　consoled each day
　　by your soft tickled arms
　　dancing each day
　　to your electric heart beats
　　thankful to live in a world
　　that allows me to say
　　hello
　　each day
to you

Vows

wedding bells, black tie optional
a string quartet creating harmonies that
fuse single tones into art
vowing to never understand
love
or art
vowing to live each day
clumsily experimenting
until volcanoes erupt
leaving footprints
permanently emblazoned
on a snowy canvas

- love and art are created, not found

I Do

when they said
she looks beautiful
i knew they saw you
like i do

when they said
to the happy couple
i knew they saw us
like i do

when you said
nice to meet you
i overthought things
like i do

but

when you said
i love you
i knew we'd say things
like *i do*

First Dance

four left feet
freely frolicked on the floor

four eyes meet
seeing what they had in store

four four beat
time in common to explore

'fore, deplete
now i want for nothing more

Under the Greenwood Tree

we lie
under the greenwood tree
the echoes of our youth
fall lightly on the horizon
the spirit of the sun
attempting to break through
the canopy
but
we lie
bold and still
the breeze
soothing our bodies
reminding us
of our idle nature
let it satisfy
in this moment
separate, yet connected
content
we lie

I Went to Look for Joy

i went to look for sorrow
in endless longing for tomorrow

i went to look for hate
in selfish words and harsh debate

i went to look for greed
in coins that cut and bills that bleed

i went to look for fear
in friendships only built on beer

i went to look for pain
in starting all over again

but then…

i went to look for hope
in a kiss-sealed envelope

i went to look for love
in a hand that fit my glove

i went to look for life
in a fun and caring wife

i went to look for joy
in a healthy girl and boy

i went to look for me
and found myself in family

It Takes a Moment

sometimes it takes a moment
sometimes it takes a life
sometimes it takes a moment to realize what is
    important in life
sometimes it takes a moment to realize what is
    important in a wife
sometimes it takes a wife
sometimes it takes a wife to realize what is important in
    life
sometimes a moment with a wife is the most important
    moment in a life
a moment with you is the most important moment in my
    life
thank you for being my wife
thank you for being my life

10

We Live

Through darkest dusk and brightest dawn
We find the strength to carry on
Run side by side, a marathon
To last a life

Farther than we ever ran
Beyond our most indulgent plan
Side by side, I am your man
With you, my wife

And so…

I lived.
You lived.
We both lived

          together.
          for each other.
          happily ever after.

We lived.
We lived and lived and lived.

We lived to create a life worthwhile.
From the moment we walked down the aisle,
Hand in hand, lips in smile,
Giggling, acting juvenile,
Time stood still, a blank sundial.
My grape turned me to oenophile.

The taste of life, so satisfying.
You lift me up and now I'm flying.
And yet, your gravity's intensifying.
You draw me in, it's mystifying.
One thing is certain, there's no denying.
Whatever you sell, I'm always buying.

Therefore…

Lead the way, down an endless road
I'll always stay to lighten your load
I'll always say that I followed
The brightest ray the sun bestowed

Here

have no fear
i'll be here
for every tear
through every year

Burnt Toast

true love isn't
toasting your bread on level five
even when i know
level four is better

true love is
knowing the joyful smile
you get from eating
burnt toast
and
setting it on fire
just for you

Candy Lovers

we are two
candy lovers
sweetness surprising
our twirling tongues
content to share a bowl
of candy-coated happiness
i'll take the m's
you can have the w's

Muse

i've been swimming in a drought of thought
can't help sinking and i doubt a lot
the words won't come, so the pen still stalls
i'm feeling trapped behind ten steel walls
when she'll call, i hope she stays the night
put the words to the paper by the morning light
if i lose my muse, i might just go insane
'cause with her by my side, the ink pours like rain

Staycation

how far must we travel
        to find our way home
trudging through gravel
        through river, through loam
crossroads unravel
        return to our station
back in our saddle
        with you, it's staycation

Only You

i will lose my mind for you
until i cannot recall
where or why or how or when
only who
only you

Anti-Religion

you are my anti-religion
who needs faith
when you show me
every day
how omnipotent love can be

Lazy Morning

the sunlight streaks our love-stained walls
the scent of coffee lingers
the sporadic song of childhood calls
the day slips through our fingers

Trying to Speak

the flowery words i put to page
don't make up for the
sounds of emotional silence
you've had to endure
i'm trying to unleash my voice
but it is hoarse from disuse
lean in a little closer
to hear the man in me wake up

Dilly

i love to dally with my dilly
leading lives so light and silly
kissing lips of sweet chantilly
knowing everything's alright

let's just be and dilly-dally
rolling gently down the alley
striking contrast from the valley
mountains rising to take flight

Shuffle, Repeat

as i awoke this evening
to a world we built together
i hear our music playing
note for note, key for key

the songs composed in times
when we had the strength to write them
and now we draw our strength
from the joyful moments they contain

we both know every word
each inflection in the vocals
so deep are the ear-worms
that they play throughout our sleep

we hum the tunes together
as we lay beside each other
content to let the record
continue playing on repeat

and when the day is over
we will play it once again
knowing that this album
contains all our favourite songs

Our House

we built this house
our life's vignette
on concrete vows
foundations set
we fastened seams
with sweat and strength
the marbled beams
all cut to length
our calloused fingers
traced the walls
our scent still lingers
through the halls
our footsteps rocked
the floors to slumber
our hearts unlocked
like swinging lumber
our numbers grew
through tight embrace
we always knew
we'd leave this place
our lives transposed
forced to evict
the doors now closed
the windows bricked
our home still stands
strong and firm
built by love
for a lifelong term

Tide

we used to chase tsunamis
pretending we were giants
now we bury ourselves in the
warm sand, awaiting low tide

Epilogue

A Poem You'll (hopefully) Never Read

your scars sear my skin
the scents of burning flesh
replace the freshness of our love
apothecary vices calm and erase the memories
literary devices provide the space to understand the pain
when you went   away
you left nothing but an inner vacuum of outer space
floating never felt so **heavy**
f r e e d o m never felt so constricted
a gift with a black bow
tied too tightly around my neck
what's the point of air
when there's no one there to share it
what's the point of breath
when there's no one there to take it away

10 (Devoted Decade)

dear bunny
in the summery yard
    where the sweat-planted hydrangeas grow
    where the emerald grass cuts our feet
    forever greener than the neighbours'
    rock garden
    blades sharp, despite your flats
    exfoliating deeper than the decade devoted
    to the trail of bloody breadcrumbs that
mark our home

mark our home
    with words
the ones we spoke those years ago
the ones that spoke of waterfalls
    bungee cords lying slack by the cliff
    parachutes from toile doilies
    dotting sunburns on our backs
the ones that spoke of dinosaurs
    those lovely bones discovered
    digging deeper than the decade devoted
    to finding fortune
    those diamonds
    blood stained glass windows
    rainbows crying *sanctuary!*
    as midnight snowflakes claim
the earth

the earth
from space, still special
    the precious little diamond
    fading, worn out, weathered
    still collecting sun to warm
us, the lucky *Ones*
as we recover from the shivering
shelter-in-place of absolute *Zero*
burning bunkers made of gold
    that stories told of long ago
and with a melted heart
    filled with spreadsheets
    full of sounds
    from the devoted decade
    filed deep inside my silent soul
and with a balance owing
    despite the centenary tithe
let us sit here in the yard
until the taxman dares collect

Jordan Littman

Special Thanks

To Keely: You have been the inspiration behind this book, but you also inspire me to be a better person every day. Thank you for your undying support, regardless of how crazy my projects may seem. This book is proof that, occasionally, I do finish a project!

To the reader: If you have made it this far, I want to let you know how deeply honoured I am that you have taken the time from your busy day to spend it reading my words. I hope you have gained something valuable from it, whether a piece of wisdom, a smile, or simply a short period of relaxation. Your ongoing support is greatly appreciated!

Index

About the Author

Dr. Jordan Littman lives in Ottawa, Canada, with his wife and two children. He has enjoyed writing poetry and songs since he was a young child and has recently returned to these roots as a way to break up the busy day working as a family physician, owning a local Escape Room business and developing iOS apps. *Perfection: 10 Years of Love* is his first collection of poetry.

FOLLOW ON SOCIAL MEDIA

Instagram: @a.mind.unsorted

Facebook: Jordan Littman Poetry

Printed in Great Britain
by Amazon